KU-026-089

GALWAY COUNTY LIBRARIES

WITHDRAWN FROM CIRCULATION

GALWAY COUNTY LIBRARIES

Prokofiev

Wendy Lynch

First published in Great Britain by Heinemann Library,
Halley Court, Jordan Hill, Oxford OX2 8EJ,
a division of Reed Educational and Professional Publishing Ltd.
Heinemann is a registered trademark of Reed Educational & Professional Publishing Limited.

OXFORD MELBOURNE AUCKLAND
JOHANNESBURG BLANTYRE GABORONE
IBADAN PORTSMOUTH NH (USA) CHICAGO

© Reed Educational and Professional Publishing Ltd 2000

The moral right of the proprietor has been asserted.

All rights reserved. No part of this publication may be reproduced, stored in a retrieval system, or transmitted in any form or by any means, electronic, mechanical, photocopying, recording, or otherwise without either the prior written permission of the Publishers or a licence permitting restricted copying in the United Kingdom issued by the Copyright Licensing Agency Ltd, 90 Tottenham Court Road, London W1P OLP.

Designed by Visual Image
Illustrations by Shirley Bellwood
Originated by Dot Gradations
Printed and bound in Hong Kong/China

04 03 02 01 00
10 9 8 7 6 5 4 3 2 1

ISBN 0 431 02308 5

GALWAY COUNTY LIBRARIES

British Library Cataloguing in Publication Data

Lynch, Wendy
Prokofiev. – (Lives and times)
1. Prokofiev, S. S. (Sergei Sergeevich), 1891–1953 – Juvenile literature
2. Composers – Soviet Union – Biography – Juvenile literature
I. Title
780.9'2
ISBN 0431023085

J182772 £14.00
920/PRO

Acknowledgements

The Publishers would like to thank the following for permission to reproduce photographs: AKG London: pp17, 23 (main pic); Haddon Davies: pp20, 21; Novosti (London): pp15, 16, 22, 23 (inset); Prokofiev Archive: p19.

Cover photograph reproduced with permission of AKG London.

Every effort has been made to contact copyright holders of any material reproduced in this book. Any omissions will be rectified in subsequent printings if notice is given to the Publisher.

For more information about Heinemann Library books, or to order, please phone ++44 (0)1865 888066, or send a fax to ++44 (0)1865 314091. You can visit our website at www.heinemann.co.uk.

Any words appearing in the text in bold, **like this**, are explained in the Glossary.

Contents

Early life

Sergei Prokofiev was born in Sontsovka, Russia, on 23 April 1891. At night, when he lay in bed, he loved to hear his mother playing the piano.

GALWAY COUNTY LIBRARIES

When Sergei was five years old his mother taught him how to play the piano. He also began to make up his own music. This is called **composing**.

Composing

By 1904 Sergei had written a **symphony**, four **operas** and many pieces of music for the piano. He also loved to play **chess**.

When he was twelve Sergei went to study music in St Petersburg, Russia. It was difficult for Sergei to make friends because all the other students were much older than him.

Travel

Sergei worked very hard at **composing** music. People did not always like his music because it sounded strange to them. But in 1914 he won a competition playing his own music.

Sergei travelled in Europe and the USA. In New York, he wrote an **opera** called *The Love for Three Oranges*. Many people liked it and Sergei became famous.

Marriage

When Sergei was 29 he went to live in Paris. Here he married a woman called Lina and they had two sons. Sergei's mother also came to live with them.

In 1927 Sergei went on a **tour** of Russia to play his music. His tour was very successful. This made Sergei feel **homesick**. In 1936 he and his family went to live in Russia.

Peter and the Wolf

In 1936 Sergei wrote *Peter and the Wolf*. Sergei wanted to help children learn the different musical instruments in an **orchestra**. So he wrote a story about a boy called Peter.

 The Bird by the Flute

The Duck by the Oboe

The Cat by the Clarinet

 The Wolf by the French Horn

Every **character** in *Peter and the Wolf* is played by a different instrument. In the story, Peter meets a bird, a duck, a cat and a wolf!

GALWAY COUNTY LIBRARIES

Last days

Sergei wrote a **ballet** called *Romeo and Juliet* in 1940. But now it became difficult for him to write music as he wanted. The ruler of Russia did not like Sergei's music.

Sergei **composed** music every day of his life, even when he was travelling and there was no piano and no desk. He became ill and died on 5 March 1953.

Photos and paintings

There are many ways in which we can find out about Sergei Prokofiev. People took a lot of photos of him. Here is a photo of Sergei as a baby with his mother and father.

Many artists did drawings and paintings of Sergei. Here is a **portrait** of him that was painted in 1934.

Letters and manuscripts

Sergei travelled the world. This is a poster for a **concert** he played in Spain in 1935. He wrote many letters when he was away from home.

Asociación de
Cultura Musical

MADRID

AÑO 15   1935·1936   Concierto 3

SERGE
PROKOFIEFF

PIANISTA

Here is a **manuscript** written by Sergei.
It shows how he wrote music on a page.
He wrote some music as a birthday
present for his old music teacher.

Music

There are many ways in which you can hear Prokofiev's music. You can go to a **concert** or you can listen to a CD like this one of *Peter and the Wolf*.

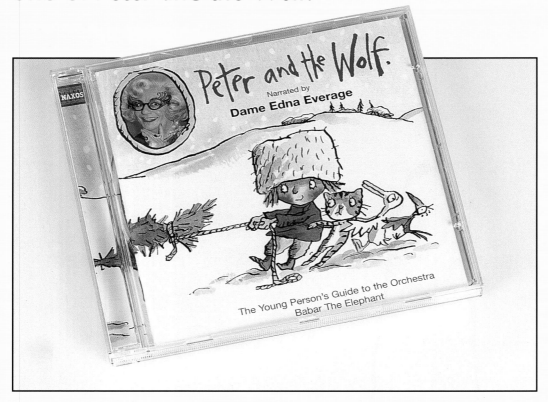

J182,772

Sergei's music is still very popular. This book tells the story of *Peter and the Wolf*.

GALWAY COUNTY LIBRARIES

Remembering Prokofiev

We can find out many things about Sergei Prokofiev's life and music. This picture shows what the costumes looked like for his **opera** *The Love for Three Oranges*.

Prokofiev's wife, Lina, helped to start the Prokofiev **Archive** in London. Here you can see books, films, letters and newspapers about Sergei. These mean that he will always be remembered.

Glossary

This glossary explains difficult words, and helps you to say words which may be hard to say.

archive place to keep a lot of information together. You say *ar-kyve*.

ballet play full of dancing. You say *bal-ay*.

character game played on a chequered board

chess person in a story. You say *ka-rak-ter*.

compose make up music

concert public show by musicians or singers. You say *kon-sert*.

homesick wanting to be at home

manuscript music written by hand. You say *man-you-script*.

opera play full of songs

orchestra large group of musicians who play their musical instruments together. You say *or-kes-tra*.

portrait picture that looks just like a person's face. You say *paw-trayt*.

symphony a long piece of music (in three or four parts) for many musical instruments. You say *sim-fun-ee*.

tour a long journey to different countries. You say *taw*.

GALWAY COUNTY LIBRARIES

Index

GALWAY COUNTY LIBRARIES